Up in space

Mercury

and Venus

Rosalind Mist

Editor: Lauren Taylor
Designer: Melissa Alaverdy
Educational consultants:
    Heather Adamson
    and Jillian Harker

Copyright © QED Publishing,
2013

First published in the UK by
QED Publishing,
A Quarto Group Company
6 Blundell Street
London N7 9BH

www.qed-publishing.co.uk

ISBN 978 1 78171 213 9

Printed in China

A catalogue record for this
book is available from the
British Library.

Picture credits
(fc=front cover, t=top,
b=bottom, l=left, r=right,
c=centre)

NASA fc, NASA JPL/USGS 1b, Johns
Hopkins University Applied Physics
Laboratory/Carnegie Institution of
Washington 2-3, NASA JPL/USGS
18b, Johns Hopkins University
Applied Physics Laboratory/
Carnegie Institution of Washington
22-33, NASA JPL/USGS 24
Science Photo Library Chris
Butler 8-9, Walter Meyers 9t, Chris
Butler 10-11, 12-13, NASA 14-15,
cy 16-17,
ay 18-19,
ard Slawik 20-
rtini Sabor 1t,
alchuk 18b,
ear in the
24.

Contents

Mercury

Mercury is the closest **planet** to the Sun. It is also the smallest planet in the **Solar System**. Mercury is dry and rocky. There are holes all over it. These are called **craters**.

craters

4

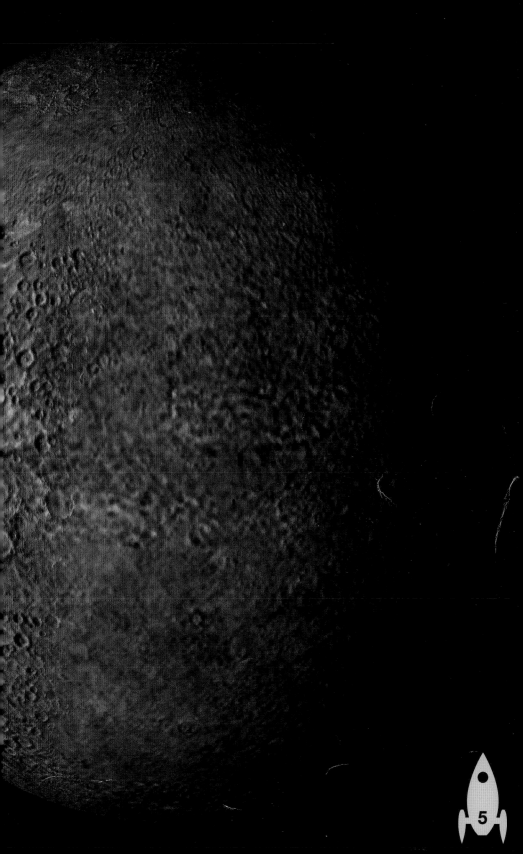

The Solar System

The Solar System is made up of the Sun and all the things that go around it.

Mars

Earth

Venus

Mercury

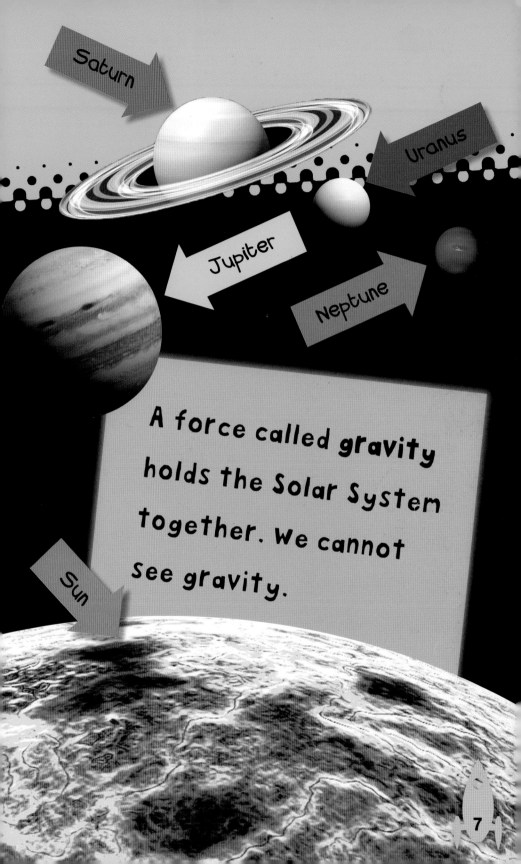

Saturn

Uranus

Jupiter

Neptune

A force called **gravity** holds the Solar System together. We cannot see gravity.

Sun

Hot and Cold

Mercury is close to the Sun. It gets very hot in the daytime. But it cannot hold any heat. Mercury gets very cold at night.

daytime

night-time

A day

Mercury spins slowly.
A day on Mercury is
176 Earth days.

Mercury

Sun

Craters

There are craters all over Mercury. Many were made when the planet was hit by asteroids or comets.

Crater

Some craters were
made by volcanoes.

Exploring the planets

Scientists use **Space probes** to explore the planets. Probes can fly past or land on the surface. Two probes have visited Mercury so far.

Mercury

14

space probe

Venus

Venus is the second
planet from the
Sun. It is about the
same size as the
Earth. But Venus
looks very
different.

Venus was the first
planet to be visited
by a space probe.

16

Hot surface

Venus has a layer
of gases around it.
This holds in a lot of
the sun's heat.

gases

Venus gets very hot!

19

Crossing the Sun

Sometimes Venus
passes between the
Earth and the Sun.

Sun

When Venus crosses
the Sun it can be
seen from Earth.

Earth

Volcanoes

Venus has a lot of volcanoes. It has more than any other planet in the Solar System.

The biggest volcano on Venus is 8 kilometres high.

volcanoes

Glossary

asteroids – small rocky objects that move around the Sun

comet – a chunk of ice and dirt that moves around the Sun in a long path

crater – a hole in the ground caused by something falling or by a volcano

gravity – the force that pulls things towards each other

planet – one of the eight large objects circling the Sun

solar system – the Sun and all of the things that move around it

space probe – an unmanned vehicle used to explore space

volcano – a mountain through which melted rock, ash and hot gases sometimes erupt